MEMOIRS OF MICHAEL:

The Hurricane Project

MEMOIRS OF MICHAEL:

The Hurricane Project

Ashley Conner
Cierra Camper

Copyright © 2019 Ashley Conner and Cierra Camper.

All rights reserved. No part of this book may be reproduced, stored, or transmitted by any means—whether auditory, graphic, mechanical, or electronic—without written permission of the author, except in the case of brief excerpts used in critical articles and reviews. Unauthorized reproduction of any part of this work is illegal and is punishable by law.

Because of the dynamic nature of the Internet, any web addresses or links contained in this book may have changed since publication and may no longer be valid. The views expressed in this work are solely those of the author and do not necessarily reflect the views of the publisher, and the publisher hereby disclaims any responsibility for them.

Any people depicted in stock imagery provided by Getty Images are models,
and such images are being used for illustrative purposes only.
Certain stock imagery © Getty Images.

Scriptures taken from the Holy Bible, New International Version®, NIV®. Copyright © 1973, 1978, 1984, 2011 by Biblica, Inc.™ Used by permission of Zondervan. All rights reserved worldwide. www.zondervan.com The "NIV" and "New International Version" are trademarks registered in the United States Patent and Trademark Office by Biblica, Inc.™

ISBN: 978-0-578-22183-0 (sc)
ISBN: 978-1-6847-1382-0 (hc)
ISBN: 978-1-6847-1380-6 (e)

Library of Congress Control Number: 2019918673

Lulu Publishing Services rev. date: 12/04/2019

Write what should not be forgotten.
—Isabell Allende

    To the memoirees: thank you for allowing me to write about one of the most challenging seasons of your life. Cierra, thank you for dedicating countless hours to this project. To my husband and our two daughters, who were the greatest source of love and support throughout this project, thank you and I love you.

—A. C.

    To the memoirees: thank you for trusting me and opening your homes for me to document authentically. I know it wasn't easy to relive it and I appreciate your willingness more than anything. To my family and Josh: thank you for supporting me while I worked endless hours and protecting me while I traveled to unknown locations and homes. To Ashley: thank you for including me in this life-changing project; it's a joy working alongside you.

—C. C.

PREFACE

On April 25, 2015, a deadly earthquake hit Nepal, devastating the country's infrastructure and killing nearly nine thousand people. Less than a week later, I deployed to Nepal as an Air Force public affairs officer along with US Airmen and Marines to provide humanitarian assistance. Before landing at the Kathmandu airport, I read every post-earthquake news article I could get my hands on. Other countries were being accused of taking advantage of Nepal's devastation to bolster their own reputation. On Twitter, the hashtag #GoHomeIndiaMedia was trending in response to insensitive reporting. With this understanding, I was acutely aware of the communication challenges ahead of me.

On May 12, I sat down in the courtyard of the American Club to eat my lunch after taking a meeting with Joint Task Force 505 leaders. Before the 7.8-magnitude earthquake hit, the American Club was a sports and dining club for the Americans working in Nepal. The grassy areas now held big white tents filled to the brim with cots to house the US Airmen and Marines.

I watched birds happily picking at dropped bread crumbs and chips. All of a sudden, the birds flew off at once as if a starting gun had fired. Then I felt why. It was another earthquake. I was seated on a stone bench, but it felt like I was on a wave. My Nepalese cell phone rang. "Hello?"

"Where are you?" I heard the familiar voice of a teammate ask.

"At the American Club."

"Stay put. We are coming to get you."

I hung up. The waves didn't stop. In the distance, I could see plumes of dust rising. I realized later that it was from the buildings falling—buildings that weeks earlier had withstood a 7.8-magnitude earthquake but gave up during this 7.3-magnitude earthquake and tumbled down.

My teammates arrived and drove me back to the airport. It was chaotic. Helicopters had been dispatched to remote villages to bring back injured Nepali citizens. One of my duties as a public affairs officer was to write news articles and take pictures. That night, there were at least five Marine combat camera photographers taking pictures of the injured as they were carried from the aircraft to the makeshift triage staging area. I knew better than to get in their way.

I saw a young girl crying. She had dark hair like my two daughters. Two days earlier was Mother's Day, and I had missed spending it with them. I could feel my heart breaking as the young Nepali girl reached toward the table where her mother was being treated. I couldn't stand around and watch. I put down my camera and asked our medical team chief where he needed me to go. "To the litter carry line," he said.

I jumped in line behind a Nepali bus driver. His gray T-shirt was covered in sweat. The first woman we carried off of a helicopter could have been my grandmother. I can remember how she smelled more than anything else: incense, dried blood, and dirt. She was curled toward me and was chanting. She reached her hand up to touch my face. The next person we carried off was a young girl. She had been stabilized and didn't look that bad. Later, I would learn internal injuries can be deadly.

In the weeks that followed, the aftershocks paralyzed me with fear. One day I was in the airport, standing near the duty-free shop. This one was full of alcohol. It all began to shake. The brown and amber liquids sloshed around in the bottles. Everyone in the airport ran outside, pushing past each other.

After I returned home only a few short weeks later, talking about my experiences helped me cope. My family and coworkers listened and would give the polite "Oh, wow" or "How scary" after I told them an abbreviated version of my time in Nepal. It would take another month before I would stop feeling earthquake tremors.

When Hurricane Michael hit on Wednesday, Oct. 10, 2018, I was sitting in a California Pizza Kitchen in Birmingham, Alabama. My family had evacuated from our home in Panama City the day before the storm hit. Watching the news coverage of the storm as it barreled toward our town was like watching a car crash in slow motion. There wasn't anything we could do but watch and pray.

Three days before making landfall Hurricane Michael was a tropical storm. Many longtime residents who had hunkered down in the Florida Panhandle for category two and three hurricanes over the years believed Hurricane Michael would be largely uneventful. At the time of landfall, Hurricane Michael was a category four but would later be upgraded to a category five. Earning a place in history as one of the strongest hurricanes to hit the continental United States.

The news coverage in the following weeks consisted of pictures and video of destroyed businesses, homes, and schools. My heart broke.

My time in Nepal prepared me for what news coverage of a natural disaster would look like. There would be weather experts weighing in, government organizations providing updates on where citizens can go for food and water, and local and state officials advocating for the necessary funding. Hurricane Michael news coverage was very similar in that regard.

In the months after the storm, everyone in Bay County had one thing in common. While standing in line at the grocery store or waiting to get a prescription filled, one would ask, "How did you fare?" With little hesitation, people's stories would tumble out. As soon as I thought I had heard the worst of it, I only had to wait until another group of friends gathered. Someone would inevitably share a hurricane story from a coworker or a sister's friend and it would be worse than the previous story.

I felt there was a gap between the news coverage and the stories I was hearing from my friends and neighbors. *Memoirs of Michael* became a passion project to help fill that gap. It was never intended to tell the worst story or the craziest story. I wanted to tell everyone's story. I wanted people to know that stories and experiences mattered. I needed that after Nepal, and I wanted to be able to give that to my community.

Photographer Cierra Camper and I spent the months after Hurricane Michael interviewing and photographing Panhandle families to tell their stories. Every story has been different and unique, but there have been a few consistent themes. Love. Once everything has been stripped away from you, you come to truly realize what really matters: your family and friends. It isn't the things but the people you love. Community. In the days, weeks, and months after Hurricane Michael, the communities impacted have come together like never before.

I hope those who chose to share their stories with us have found some healing. I hope those who randomly picked this book up in a bookstore feel, for two minutes, what some are still dealing with today. I also hope that in one hundred years, when the next big storm hits, this book provides some insight and wisdom to those who have to choose between evacuating or riding it out.

ON DUTY

His Story

I heard my wife scream. Her voice was muffled by the wind, and then the line went dead.

I had stepped back into my bedroom in the firehouse to take her call. I sat for a second with the phone in my hand, calling her name into the receiver.

I told my chief that my wife had called and needed help. He nodded. I ran into the parking lot and jumped into a truck.

The wind and rain made it impossible to see. The wind rocking the truck was going to make it hard to drive. Nearly impossible.

What if I left to find her, and something happened to me? What if she was fine, and I got hurt—or died?

I got out of the truck and fought my way back through the storm and into the firehouse.

I sat and waited. There was a low hum of voices, but everyone was somber. The gravity of how bad it was kept all of our attention.

It was the longest four hours of my life.

My shift had started that morning. We normally have five firefighters on duty. That day we had fifteen firefighters plus fifteen police officers waiting out the storm with us. There were a couple of us who had families at home. We all sat and prayed.

My family never considered evacuating. We have lived our entire lives in North Florida. We rode out many category two and three hurricanes, and this didn't seem like it would be any different. We bought supplies, boarded up our windows, and prepared for what we thought would be the worst outcome: no electricity.

After the storm passed and it was safe, I grabbed a chainsaw and rescue rope and drove to our house. I dodged trees and downed power lines, going sixty miles per hour to get to them.

Our street was blocked. I parked my truck and ran the half mile or so to our home. I couldn't run on the street because of the debris, so I ran in the ditch. The water was up to my knees, and it filled up my boots. I had to stop and let the water pour out so I could keep running.

The houses I passed on our street were intact.

Then our house came into view. The roof was gone. They were dead. I knew it, but I kept running.

I flung open the door to our home. The ceilings had fallen in. There was a mattress in the hallway, and on it sat a cat.

I ran out of the house and back out into the street.

Then I saw her. The woman I have been madly in love with for the last nineteen years and whom I have known my entire life.

She was alive.

So was our son and our friend who had been with them.

I wouldn't have cared if our entire house had fallen into a sinkhole. They were safe, and nothing else mattered.

I will never forget that moment. If you could bottle up that feeling, it would be priceless.

I hugged them. I told her that I thought that I had killed them because I didn't make them evacuate. I thought it was all my fault.

Her Story

I screamed through the phone, "Our roof is coming off!" Then the cell service dropped.

The electricity had been off for a while. Because the windows were boarded up, it was completely dark. A large tree fell beside our house, clipping the end of the roof. It began peeling off while we were in the hallway and sitting under a mattress.

We could see bright light coming in under the closed bedroom doors. The wind blew violently, shaking all the doors and windows. The ceiling in the dining room and in the bedrooms fell in, so we had a clear view of the sky for the next four hours.

Still clinging to the mattress. Sitting in several inches of water.

Honestly, I had doubts that we would make it out alive. We stayed calm and prayed a lot.

We had gotten up that morning at 5:00 a.m. and checked the weather. I immediately knew something was wrong because the weatherman was broadcasting live. He looked like he was going to vomit. Obviously, things had grown significantly worse overnight. They said, "If you haven't left at this point, stay put and hunker down." So we did.

My husband went to work while I stayed home with our fifteen-year-old son and my friend who lives in an apartment by herself.

Around 4:00 p.m., the wind started to calm down. We heard voices and a dog barking outside. I made my way through the house and over to our neighbor's house. Then through their window, I could see my husband, still in his firefighter bunker gear, racing up the street. I ran out of our neighbors' front door with my son and friend behind me. I hugged him hard. I hadn't cried through the entire ordeal, and now it all came out. So many tears. I had never been so happy to see him in my entire life. It was absolutely the happiest moment. This whole situation was worse for him. There was no cell service, so we couldn't get in touch with him. He didn't know whether we were alive or not.

We bought a camper to live in while we rebuild. We enjoy every single day that we have been blessed with.

We had an amazing group of New York City Fire Department volunteers from a nonprofit organization called Heart 9/11 come help us completely gut our house.

People continue to say, "I'm so sorry about your house."

I tell them, "Don't be sorry, because I'm not. I'm just happy to be alive and have my family and friends safe."

When you peel away all the material things and only have each other left, you realize that's all that ever really mattered to begin with.

We will watch the next hurricane that comes on a television from a hotel room far, far away.

MICHAEL'S MOONWALK

Michael came through and did the moonwalk. He didn't pick and choose. He hit everyone.

A long time ago, I did roofing. I had appendix surgery and had complications. That was the end of my work.

I lived in a trailer with my daughter and her son. When the hurricane was coming, I sent them away. I stayed. The trees fell, and the whole trailer was destroyed. I was sleeping under a tarp with my dog when some nice people came by and helped me get a FEMA trailer.

The stairs on the trailer were too steep for me to climb, so the same nice people came back and built me a ramp. I don't have anything, so I am happy with anything people give me. I am eighty-one years old. All I want is to see my daughter and her son doing well.

WE HAVE A FLAT ROOF—OR HAD

We have a flat roof—or had. We had a flat roof.

It sounded like someone was stomping on it, and then the whole roof peeled back.

It was raining all around us.

The kids and I went into a small hallway outside our bedroom and stayed there until the ceiling in the living room fell in. We went downstairs to the middle of our house and waited out the storm.

I cried as I watched the hurricane destroy the home we had spent the last ten years building. I cried that my children were in this situation.

My nineteen-year-old daughter was a rock during the entire storm. She helped her eleven-year-old sister and three-year-old brother stay calm by singing them songs. My three-year-old had a bucket of treats that he clung to for dear life. He ate continuously until we told him to stop. A stomachache during the midst of a hurricane was the last thing we needed.

My husband and my brother-in-law were busy assessing the situation. They made sure we were safe. We went upstairs a few times in the midst of the storm, and we were able to salvage some clothes and our wedding photos.

My husband is a man of many trades. He does all types of work: car audio, closed-circuit television, merchant services, pool service, solar paneling installation, and remodeling. You name it, and he can do it—or he will learn how. We have been fortunate that he has had lots of work since the storm.

We won't stay for another hurricane. I'm glad we were here, though. It helped us understand the magnitude of the hurricane and the destruction it brought.

We will do what it takes to get things back to normal, or as normal as possible. We have grown in a lot of ways. I think we are closer—closer to God and to each other.

MEMOIRS OF MICHAEL: THE HURRICANE PROJECT

HURRICANE A-TEAM

The waiting room doors to the emergency department at Bay Medical were the first to blow out. The ambulance bay doors started to rattle. We were afraid they were going to blow out too.

I am an emergency medicine physician at Bay Medical Center at the main hospital and at the Panama City Beach Emergency Room.

When the hurricane warning and evacuation notices went out, I got confirmation that I was scheduled to work my three-day "hurricane A-team" shifts from Tuesday until Thursday.

My husband was on call that week as a plastic surgeon for the hospital, so we

decided we would both stay at the hospital. We sent our children to stay with family in Alabama.

There was very little time for me to prepare for the hurricane or even pack appropriately before heading off to the hospital on Tuesday morning.

When I arrived for my shift, everyone was nervous but optimistic. It was only a category one, possibly two, storm.

I worked all day Tuesday, and we went to sleep that night on an inflatable mattress on the floor of an empty patient room. When we woke up the day of the hurricane, we learned that it had strengthened into a category four hurricane. We were going to be hit hard.

We had patients in the ER that morning, and the hospital had more than two hundred patients on the floors. When the storm hit, we moved all the ER patients to the most central part of the department. The staff congregated at the nurse's station, listening to the destruction going on outside.

Many of the windows in the hospital started cracking and breaking. Water leaked down from the ceiling, and nurses and staff frantically moved patients out of rooms and into safe areas in the hallways.

As the storm passed, we lost power and water. There was no Internet or cell service. The generator kept some of the lights and critical equipment on, but without water, we could not cool down many machines that were needed in the hospital, making them unusable.

A rush of patients came in shortly after the storm passed. Although the ER's front door was damaged, we never closed. People started to come in by foot or were driven in by people with trucks that could make it over the debris.

It was chaotic.

We were trying to take care of patients without computers, labs, or running water and with limited X-ray capability.

The hospital started to evacuate patients after the hurricane hit. Staff were able to transfer more than two hundred patients to other hospitals within forty-eight hours after the storm hit. Not a single patient, staff, or their family members were hurt during the hurricane.

After working fourteen hours, I was exhausted. I waded through two inches of water in the hallway to get to my room.

Thursday was more of the same. My husband and I finally left the hospital Thursday evening. We could not believe the destruction to the hospital, the surrounding neighborhood, and the entire city. I cried on the way home.

I could not recognize any of the landmarks or buildings that I have driven past every day over the last seven years. It was a completely different city. I cried even more when we got home.

I cried because our city now looks like a war zone.

I cried because so many had lost so much, but our house was okay. I felt guilty.

This has been one of the most devastating events I have ever lived through.

The damages to the hospital mean the community has lost a critical resource.

The loss of hundreds of jobs at the hospital is heartbreaking. Although I understand the reason, it is very difficult to know that so many are without jobs when they have lost so much already.

I have also witnessed so much good. I am in awe of the resilience and strength of the people here. I have faith that this will not keep us down. We will rebuild and will be even better than before.

NOT A HURRICATION

At first, it felt like a vacation. We stayed in a hotel room in a new city. We went out to restaurants for every meal.

My mom and dad were always on their phones. I knew they were helping people, but sometimes I needed to tell them things.

My sister wouldn't sleep in the bunk beds at the rental house. She was afraid that the top bunk would fall on her and that Mom and Dad would be too busy on their phones to save her.

I had a dream my teacher was still in our school. She was trapped and couldn't get out. My mom let me call and talk to her. She is safe.

I am at a new school now. I have one friend. I have a good day when the teachers don't yell.

But I just want to go back to my house and my school. My mom says maybe soon.

I told her I didn't want to be here anymore. She asked me where I wanted to go. I said heaven. My mom cried and held me for a long time.

My mom and dad aren't on their phones that much anymore. We play board games every night.

Pictionary is my favorite.

IT'S GONE. ALL GONE.

Our entire house was destroyed.

We almost didn't evacuate. My husband came home from a work trip in the last seat available on the last flight back into Panama City before the hurricane hit. He walked in the door and said, "We are leaving." I had pretty bad morning sickness and wasn't as productive as I could have been about evacuating.

After the storm hit, our neighbors called us. Their cell service was spotty, but they were able to tell us our house was totaled. Three days after the storm, we were able to access the main roads to drive in and see our home.

I walked aimlessly around the debris of our house, not knowing what to think or feel. My husband's first reaction was to immediately start pulling things out of the house. Thank goodness he did, because he was able to save our wedding photos and some very sentimental things.

My doctor's office was closed, so I didn't have any appointments for a month.

I had some stress-related pregnancy issues right after the hurricane hit, but I am doing better now. My family and friends have been so supportive. We have received many care packages and clothes. Both of my kids have full closets of clothes now because of the donations from all of our wonderful friends.

I try to stay positive most of the time, but there are days that the reality of our situation hits me. I let myself have those down days too. It's a roller coaster of emotions, and we are taking it day by day. Rebuilding is a long process, and I need to remind myself of that every so often.

Overall, I feel blessed that my family is safe. Really, that is all that matters.

THE EYE

The eye sat over our house in Callaway for about fifteen minutes.

Our neighbor's house across the street had fallen in, so my husband took the opportunity during the calm to see if anyone was inside. Thankfully, they had evacuated.

When the hurricane started, we thought my son's room would be the safest. Once the winds began, it was clear that room was not safe. Just as my family of four ran into the hallway on our way to the bathroom, a tree pushed through the window of my son's room.

We put both kids in the bathtub and filled it with pillows. I could see my son's door bending and flexing, the wind trying to blow it open. I am convinced God was holding that door shut to protect us. I prayed for God to spare my family. I hid the tears rolling down my cheeks from my daughter and son. My husband stood guard at the bathroom door, making sure it stayed shut and we were safe.

As the eye of the hurricane passed over us, we could see a gray mass moving toward us. We huddled back into the bathroom as the backside of the hurricane moved over our home. It was worse than the first half. It was loud and violent and lasted three hours. We could hear the wind blowing debris against our house, shaking windows and doors. The whole house was shaking even our pipes and toilet.

The worst part after the storm was not having any cell service. There was no way of knowing whether our family and friends were safe. We drove to my parents' neighborhood, and they were airlifting injured residents out. My heart sank. Was it our family? There was no way of knowing. We parked the truck and walked the mile or so into the neighborhood. We made it to their house, and they were safe.

The next stop we made was to Holy Nativity Episcopal School, where I work. The school has loved on so many of Panama City's children over the last sixty years.

My husband and I surveyed the damage and reported back to Judy Hughes, head of the school. Over the next two weeks, Judy and I would sit together in our cars and under the damaged pavilion, mapping out our plan to get the children back into school.

It was no small feat, but we did it. Once we got everyone back together, we realized how important it was to resume some kind of normalcy—as much for the children as it was for the teachers and staff.

I have lived here for thirty-three years. This is home. I think we have a real opportunity to bring back Panama City, Callaway, Lynn Haven, and Parker (as well as the other smaller areas) in a big way. I think when we are finished, Bay County will shine like a brand-new penny!

SEPARATED, DISPLACED, AND CHANGED FOREVER

We watched hundreds of roof shingles and whole tree limbs fly by as the storm approached. We rode out the storm in my boyfriend's sister's fourth-floor apartment. The apartment building was shaking, vibrating, and swaying in the wind.

Inside the apartment, it got really hot. Hot is not a fun temperature for a pregnant woman of thirty-six weeks.

The wind and rain blew through the crack in the door. There was water everywhere, running out of the air-conditioning vent in the ceiling. Out of the light fixtures. Out of the ceiling

in the living room. And then from the bedroom ceiling. We had pots collecting water throughout the apartment. This went on for hours.

It eventually stopped, and we went outside. Every tree was down. It was like a bomb had gone off.

That night, a police officer rode through the apartment complex to let everyone know there was a citywide curfew. We asked him how it looked. He said, "The whole city is destroyed." We hoped he was exaggerating.

The next morning, we saw for ourselves. Homes were covered in trees, ripped apart and shredded by the wind.

It was a surreal sight that took my breath away.

We turned down a familiar street and saw the public housing apartment complex ripped apart. A group of ten people, including small children, were walking. We drove them across town to a shelter. We all cried the whole ride. I couldn't believe my eyes. It's a ride I will never forget.

Mobile homes lay on their side, homes were destroyed, and every church and school we saw was ravaged.

The mobile home I was renting was completely covered in trees and had several large tree limbs through the roof. The ceiling had fallen in. Most of our possessions were damaged and ruined. We salvaged some clothing and photos, but we had to abandon everything else.

I was brought to Tallahassee to have our baby.

Our son was born October 31, happy and healthy twenty-one days after Michael changed our lives.

I am staying in transitional housing for pregnant women and women who have small children. My fourteen-year-old son stayed with his father for a week or so. The community lacked the basic necessities, so they were forced to go to Texas to stay with family.

Separated and displaced, we are changed forever.

SAVING THE FAMILY HOME

The winds were so strong, our front door was blowing open. My dad held it shut with a cooler and a mini fridge. We used weights to keep the other doors shut.

Meanwhile, my mom and I were collecting the water that was pouring in.

Our damage was isolated to 150 square feet of the ceiling. If we had not been there, gallons of water would have soaked into the carpet and walls after the winds whipped the doors open.

Since the storm, my biggest struggle has been time management. I had a plethora of folks asking for help getting trees off of houses, clearing paths to the

road, and getting roofs tarped. Our family may not be professionals, but our tarps are holding up.

It was crazy balancing all the requests.

Now, I'm working full time and getting business stuff taken care of. It's challenging to accomplish everything in a day.

I have lived in Panama City my entire life. This is my home. Leaving would be like betraying it.

If it wasn't for my school and church experiences and people investing in me, I wouldn't be who I am.

As the community rebuilds, I hope residents, business owners, churches, and local government can become more forward thinking than in years past. We need to look for ways to improve this great area. We need to provide opportunities to grow.

SAVING THE FAMILY HOME

BOUNTY OF THE BAY CHARTER

My husband and our friend climbed over mounds of debris made out of boats and destroyed homes that had been washed off of their foundations. There, they found it: the top floor of our town house, one hundred yards or so away from where it belonged.

They made their way inside, and everything was perfectly intact. On the night stand, there was a gum wrapper and an iPad, just as my daughter had left it the week before. It seemed completely oblivious to the 155-mile-per-hour winds that had destroyed the rest of the house.

It was eerie.

Anything on the ground was destroyed, but we were able to save things stored in the shelves above the closet. My daughter and son's baby books and some shoes.

Where our house originally sat, we found a pile of rubble. I had set two sandbags at the front door and four at the backdoor before we evacuated. The sandbags were still there, but all that was left of the house was a slab of concrete, tile in the entryway and kitchen, and a dishwasher.

There was a two-foot waterline mark on the wall of the top floor of our town house.

The first floor of our town home had ten-foot ceilings. This means the water from the hurricane that rushed in was at least twelve-feet high.

My husband and I grew up in Panama City and later moved to Port St. Joe. We own a fishing business called Bounty of the Bay Charters in Mexico Beach. When a town home on the canal in Mexico Beach became available to rent, we took it. It meant that we could be closer to work.

We unpacked our last box October 8. Later that night, we evacuated.

It wasn't an easy decision to go. My husband wanted to stay. His whole life was here. Mine was too, but I wanted to make sure our daughter was safe.

We were expecting a big storm surge, so we tied the boat up in a way that it would rise with the tide. We grabbed a few changes of clothes and drove to Mississippi. Had we known we were going to lose everything, we would have taken more things.

The charter fishing business was our life. Last year was our best season, ever. We made a little money and met some amazing people. Our boat is stacked up among the debris behind the canal in Mexico Beach. It was the biggest boat we had ever owned. It will take a crane operator to get it out.

This has been especially hard for my husband. What is a fisherman without his boat?

I had a little money from FEMA, and I found a boat for sale. A very kind police officer sold it to me for half the price he was asking. I trailered the boat home myself and surprised my husband. He cried. I cried.

A rental home just became available in Port St. Joe. It is way more than we can afford, but we took it. I just want a roof over our heads. I just want us to get back to normal. Or find a new normal, at least.

We have appreciated every little bit of good fortune that has come our way since Hurricane Michael destroyed everything we had.

My husband has a job and works hard every single day. The business where I work will open again soon. My daughter is staying busy with school and track. This has been rough, and it has taken its toll on our family. I tell myself we will get through this.

When people say you can't cry anymore, it's BS. You can.

BE PREPARED TO LOSE EVERYTHING AT LEAST ONCE

If you live on the water, be prepared to lose everything you own at least once in your lifetime. That's what we always heard.

When Hurricane Opal hit Pensacola, the storm surge was high, even here in Panama City. We moved off the harbor to a home more inland.

We had planned to stay for Hurricane Michael. It was our son, who lives in Enterprise, Alabama, who convinced us to leave and stay with him.

We left at 4:00 a.m.

A lot of people don't leave because they are afraid. Afraid they won't be able to get back in. Afraid of looting.

BE PREPARED TO LOSE EVERYTHING AT LEAST ONCE

My mother is eighty-five years old and lives in a nursing home nearby. She was another reason we didn't want to leave, but they ended up evacuating her before the storm hit.

We have lived in Panama City all of our lives. My husband was fifteen years old when he moved across the street from my family. We started dating two years later, and we have been together ever since. Married for forty-six years.

I can't imagine going through this without family.

This has been one of the hardest things we have ever been through. It's the hardest because we can't see the end. You know it will get better, but you can't see how.

I retired from Bay District Schools in 2015 after twenty years. My husband retired from the paper mill in 2012. He worked there for forty years. He did every job at the mill but ended his career as the pulp mill superintendent. We had a big party at the Martin House when he retired.

After the storm, WestRock, the company that owns the paper mill, gave gas, ice, and water to current and retired employees. You could go to the mill and take a hot shower or wash clothes. You don't see companies treat people like that anymore.

We shared our gas, ice, and water with our neighbors. That was one of the best things about the storm. All the fences were down. Neighbors were talking and sharing supplies. We depended on each other to get through those days.

This is not how we want to spend our retirement years, living in our camper in our driveway.

We couldn't leave, though. This is home. Our families are here.

We have had to learn to have lots of patience. Things don't move quickly. Little things take a long time. Everyone here is just moving a little bit slower.

WHO BROUGHT THE CHILI?

Someone brought chili. Of all the things to bring to a hurricane shelter, someone brought a Crockpot of chili. It was delicious.

We went to the shelter the morning the hurricane hit. There were about thirty of us. As the storm got closer, the windows blew out. A dad and son got cut up pretty badly.

The rain started coming, and the fire alarms went off. The roof ripped off, and the glass dome in the atrium lifted up.

We all huddled into the stairwell: me, my mom, my two sisters, my daughter, my boyfriend, and twenty-five other strangers.

It started to get hot in the crowded stairwell. My boyfriend and I took my sisters and my daughter to a janitor's closet on the first floor. My sisters hadn't slept well the night before, so we laid blankets down, and they went to sleep. They slept through the whole hurricane.

To pass the time, my boyfriend and I talked and tried to keep my daughter preoccupied. At the time, we assumed his home (a camper) would be long gone. I told him he could stay with me for a while if he needed to.

We watched trees through the large window get snapped in half. We speculated about what type of damage the hurricane would cause throughout town.

We didn't think it would turn out to be as bad as it did.

My boyfriend works doing drywall, and while trying to lighten the mood, we joked that after all this was over, he would have a lot more business.

My daughter danced and sang "Ring around the Rosie" over and over again while we watched the rain pour in.

She is afraid of water now. It's a battle to get her to take a bath. She cries in her sleep, but she is getting better though.

My apartment flooded. It's now covered in mold. We can't live there until it's fixed, so we have been staying with family and friends. A few weeks here, a few weeks there.

I am in an okay spot because I had savings. I am also on a scholarship. I should graduate in two years. I want to open up a Dunkin' Donuts franchise.

Right now, I am focused on making sure the necessities are covered. That holidays and my daughter's birthday feel as normal as possible. I am also focused on keeping my grades up so I can keep my scholarships.

Before the hurricane, there were things I thought were important. After the hurricane, you realize they are actually not that important at all. It'll take some time to feel normal again, but we'll make it out on the other side just fine.

THE SILVER LINING

My seventy-three-year-old grandfather held the door shut. For three hours. The wind and rain did their best to wear him down.

My two-year-old clung to me but stayed calm. We were in the hallway, and we watched water pour in from the window.

To this day, I wake up in the middle of the night with panic attacks. Some days the anxiety is unbearable. My boyfriend talks me down. He helps me stay calm.

We never thought about evacuating. I have too many family members here who were too stubborn to leave.

When it was safe, we went to my apartment, and the whole ceiling had fallen in. All of our belongings were destroyed, and black mold covered the walls. We didn't have renter's insurance.

We talked about moving. We could go to his family in the Northeast, but it is expensive, and we didn't know how long it would take to find job. So we just decided to stay.

My boyfriend does construction. He has been working ten-hour shifts six days a week. It's been crazy.

The restaurant where I work is still standing. When I saw it, I cried.

When you see so many buildings that have been destroyed, you wonder why some were spared.

My shifts have been insanely busy. We are the first place drivers hit when coming in from Mexico Beach. We have no shortage of customers. Construction workers and FEMA employees are now my regulars.

I was talking one day at work about finding a house. A customer said he had a house in St. Andrews he would sell me. We had filed a claim with FEMA and got some money we could use as a down payment. Owning a home has been our dream. I always wanted a big family and a house in which we could all feel safe.

Now we have it. I hate to say it, but it's because of the hurricane.

PATIENCE AND HUMILITY

Daughter

We wanted to move out of our trailer and into a house. I just didn't think it would happen like this.

We have never evacuated for a hurricane. If a storm looked like it was going to be bad, we would go to a shelter at a local school.

This one looked really bad. I decided to go to my boyfriend's house in Vernon, Florida. My mom finished her shift at Winn Dixie and then went to stay at my sister's apartment off Twenty-third Street. It was safer than staying in the trailer. I am glad she did.

Mother

I bought supplies. I purchased some

water, food, and one flashlight. It wasn't enough. I needed more food and water. I needed another flashlight and more batteries to keep the radio going. And baby wipes. I needed them to bathe with.

My daughter and I downloaded the walkie-talkie app onto our phones. After the power went out, it wouldn't work.

I huddled in the bathroom with two dogs, my flashlight, and the radio. The wind whistled the whole time. I had never heard anything that loud. The walls were shaking.

Over the radio, I heard that the hurricane had passed. I went out onto the balcony. The pond in the apartment complex had flooded, and a couple was kayaking.

I slept in the living room that night with the sliding door open to catch the breeze. It was hot. I had no way of telling anyone I was safe, so I just waited.

Daughter

My aunt messaged my boyfriend on Facebook and said that she had picked up my mom and was taking her home to Ebro.

My aunt followed closely behind an electrician's truck and drove through a police checkpoint. The police thought she was with them and didn't stop her from driving into town.

I got back to our trailer three days after the storm. It was destroyed. I have had the same room for twenty years, and now it is gone. I was able to save a few valuables, mementos, and some clothes. The pictures of the destruction I had seen on the news didn't do it justice. I cried.

I am living with my dad now until my mom and I can find a house or a town house in Panama City. I see my mom on the weekends, but I miss her.

We know all this happened for a reason. We need to figure out what it's trying to teach us. Patience. Humility. We can't just leave before this experience truly changes us for the better.

Next time, we will evacuate. Even if it's a tropical storm, we are gone.

LIFE IS HARD

Everything is just harder now. Our peaceful life and normal routine are permanently disrupted.

The bottom floor of our home was completely destroyed. We found the top floor completely untouched on the other side of the canal in Mexico Beach. My husband was able to bag up my work clothes and a few personal items. My husband's truck, two boats, and everything else we own is gone. All gone.

We evacuated with three dogs and two cats. I thank God that we did.

When we came back after the hurricane, we parked where Toucan's used to be and hiked and crawled to our home. Or where our home used to be.

At first you heard people say, "My house was damaged worse than yours." You don't hear that anymore. People are coming together to help each other get through this difficult time.

There has been an overwhelming amount and love and support given to us and our community. The biggest need right now is food and supplies. A lot of residents in Mexico Beach don't have cars. They have been relying heavily on donations.

We used our savings and some of the money we got from FEMA to buy a used truck and a camper.

LIFE IS HARD

The camper leaks. It is frustrating. We just want to be in a home.

There aren't any homes to rent in the area, and a lot of people are selling their land.

We don't have a routine anymore. We have to find a new normal.

But we are fighters, and we have a lot of hope.

THE DREAM

After the storm, I had a dream. My husband and I were lying in bed one night, but it wasn't our bedroom; I didn't recognize it. Then all of a sudden, the ceiling fell and landed on my husband. I will never forget what his dead body looked like in the dream.

THE DREAM

I had so much stress after that nightmare. I kept telling myself it was just a dream, but it felt so real.

We celebrated our fiftieth wedding anniversary at the end of September at our home in Mexico Beach. A few weeks later, the mandatory hurricane evacuation notices came out.

We went to Tennessee but made our way back into Mexico Beach six days after Hurricane Michael hit. As we drove back into Mexico Beach, I prayed, "Dear Lord, if you want us to have that house, let there be enough standing to rebuild. If not, then just take all of it."

We arrived at our house, or what was left of it. There was a green sticker on the door, which meant the house had been searched and no one was trapped inside.

There was six inches of mud on the ground and piles of debris over top of it.

As we walked through the house, we slipped on the mud and grabbed the walls to catch ourselves. The walls are now streaked with muddy handprints.

My husband looked at me and said, "I can fix this." He is seventy-three. He has a pacemaker and bad knees. But he is also a frame carpenter with the fierce spirit.

For the next ten days, we shoveled out the house and went to work repairing what we could. At night, we would sleep in the front of our truck. Our ankles swelled. I knew we needed to find a bed to sleep on.

We had set one of the mattresses up on wooden boards to let the water drain out. It was finally dry enough to sleep on. I drove to the Wal-Mart in Marianna and picked up some sheets. That night, we pulled the bed into a room that had little damage.

We lay down. It was glorious to have our feet propped up. Just about the time my husband fell, asleep I heard water dripping. I nudged him.

"Honey, do you hear the water dripping."

He said, "No." He is hard of hearing.

"I can. Get up."

"It's fine. Go back to sleep."

I nudged him again.

He finally sat up and told me to get a bucket. He went to use the makeshift toilet he had built out of a plastic chair and a bucket that sat in the closet. Just as he did, the ceiling fell. Sheet rock, insulation, everything fell on the bed. On his side of the bed. If he had still been lying on the bed, it would have killed him.

THE DREAM

My dream. It happened.

We went back to the truck to sleep.

In 2008, the property taxes in Mexico Beach went up drastically. We had to take a loan to pay them. We eventually ended up paying off the house, but we couldn't afford the homeowners insurance.

We have been doing all the repair work ourselves. It is hard on us at our age. We have been able to manage with the help of our children and grandchildren. We couldn't do it without them.

Team Rubicon also paid us a visit. They help veterans rebuild after a disaster. My husband retired from Tyndall Air Force Base in 1991 as a combat communications officer. It is great that organizations like that exist.

For now, we will be here working every day until the house is put back together. My birthday is three days after Christmas, and my husband made a birthday sign by stapling paper plates to the wall. We are making the best of every day the good Lord has given us.

My husband has said a couple of times, "I wish I would have let them demolish it." The good Lord saved this house for us, and I know there will be a purpose for it.

EIGHTEEN DOLLARS

I had gotten an eighteen-dollar quote for renters insurance exactly one month before the storm hit, but I never called back to finalize my enrollment. One eighteen-dollar payment, and they would have covered all the things that were damaged. We lost a lot.

I kick myself every day about that. Unfortunately for us, our landlord also didn't have any insurance on our rental property.

I lived with my boyfriend in a townhouse close to the water in St. Andrews. I worked at Uncle Ernie's. I made good money and was going to school.

I worked a double shift the Sunday before the hurricane hit. It was a holiday weekend, and we were slammed all day. We didn't even realize there was a storm until we finished our shift that night. Even then, it was just a tropical storm.

I was here for Hurricane Opal. Like a lot of locals, we didn't evacuate then either. We lived in town. We weren't under a mandatory evacuation order. We thought we were safe.

Two days before the storm, the city was chaos. Gas station lines went around the block. Most ran out by Monday afternoon. I went to the store to pick up supplies and found many empty shelves.

    You always see those people on the news hoarding supplies and buying what they think is much more than what they actually need. I didn't want to be that person. Supplies were already scarce, so I picked up only what I thought we needed.

    We woke up early Wednesday morning and quickly realized we should have left, but it was too late. If we left now, there was the fear we would be stuck out on the open roads when the storm hit.

I'll never forget the last conversation I had with my mom. She asked if we would come stay with her at her home in Forest Park. She was afraid we would fall victim to the storm surge. I told her we were going to stay put. The storm had already begun to make landfall.

She then told me in all seriousness, "Okay. Write your social security number on your arm with a Sharpie in case they need to identify your body."

My boyfriend, his mom and brother, and I hunkered down in our townhouse. We cooked our last meal on the stove and enjoyed our last moments of cable television before we lost power.

Our fence blew down within the first thirty minutes. The plywood we used to board up the windows was gone shortly after that. Almost every tree in our backyard was down within the first hour.

We moved from room to room trying to stay safe. First the living room, then the staircase, and finally settling in our downstairs bedroom. We felt safest there.

We pulled the mattress off the bed and put it against the window for extra protection. The shingles were slowly ripping off the roof. Water started pouring in through the light fixture.

We grabbed pans, bowls, and anything we could to collect the water that was now pouring in from all different parts of the ceiling. It was useless. The ceiling finally collapsed over us from the weight of the water.

We retreated back to the living room. It was the longest three hours of my life. We didn't talk much. We were lost in our own thoughts. I looked down at my stomach. Our baby was in there. I needed to stay safe.

During the middle of the storm, we somehow got a phone call from my sister. She had evacuated to Georgia and was watching the hurricane coverage live. The eye was just a couple of miles from shore, and Mexico Beach had already been wiped out.

She had called our mom. Her roof had blown off, and they were physically holding the front door shut. I felt so helpless. I burst into tears.

After it was over, we went outside. It was like a bombing in our hometown. All of our car windows had blown out. My boyfriend's truck was flooded with water. Once we drained it, we got it started and drove around. It was a sight I will never forget.

It was so hot in the days after the storm. We were sweaty and didn't shower for five days. We were underprepared. We used up all of our supplies in the first three days.

We ended up driving to a friend's house in Panama City Beach to get a shower and a hot meal. It was like a whole different world.

We are trying to stay positive and find things to celebrate. My entire family was in town for Thanksgiving, so we hosted a gender-reveal party.

When I popped the balloon, I was expecting blue or pink confetti. Instead, rhinestones came out of the balloon.

My boyfriend was down on one knee with a ring asking me to marry him. It was a happy day in the midst of all of this chaos. We eventually popped the real balloon, and blue confetti littered the ground. It's a boy, due in May.

We are currently in the market to buy a house, but we have to be patient. My only wish is that we find a home to buy or find our own place to rent before the baby is born in May.

LOVE THY NEIGHBOR

My biggest struggle has been maintaining my Christian witness while on the phone with insurance companies. Even pastors struggle.

We moved to Panama City from Port St. Joe in 2015. Our long-time Panama City neighbors had no intention of evacuating for Hurricane Michael. It gave us the confidence to stay. If the locals weren't worried, we shouldn't be either.

When it looked like the storm was going to make landfall as a category four, we decided our house, surrounded by trees, wasn't going to be safe. Along with three other families, we packed up clothes and snacks and headed to North Star Church in Panama City.

I watched the storm tracker on my phone, and about the time the west side of the eye hit, all the electricity went out.

We huddled into the church office and watched the windows bow in and out. I had never seen the wind blow that hard in my life. We moved away from the windows and into another office until rain started pouring in. We eventually ended up in the church's soundproof recording booth and rode out the rest of the storm there.

While we waited for the storm to pass, we talked about how we were going to serve the community. We wanted to hit the ground running. This building would have been ideal, but there was too much damage already.

After the storm passed and it was safe, we made our way outside. We looked down Twenty-third Street and saw an overturned semitruck. Downed power lines were everywhere. It was clear we weren't driving home.

We spent the night in the church. We hadn't planned on it, so we piled couch cushions on the floor and went to sleep in our clothes.

The next day before each family left to check on their own homes, we made a plan to check in with each other at the top of the hour using the long-range radios that the children's ministry had stored at the church.

When my family and I started driving around, it looked like a third-world country. Over the car radio, they were pleading with people to stay off the roads and evacuate even now, if possible.

We heeded their request and drove to Georgia to stay with family. After a week in Georgia, we returned to Panama City to help our community rebuild.

North Star Church set up a drive-through distribution center on the east side of town. It was pretty cool to see people pulling up their cars as we loaded them down with every kind of supply imaginable, from gas to dog food to diapers. We had it all, and the lines got longer every day.

We spent a solid two weeks working long hours distributing much-needed items. I didn't have much time to check on my own house or assess the damage, but one trip home, I found someone else had.

The tree that was on our roof was gone. The branches blocking in my car had been cut away. Tarps now covered our roof. I started calling people immediately. I needed to thank this person.

I finally found him. A North Star member owned a general contracting company, and he had sent a crew out to check on my house. "They knocked it out in no time at all," he said.

It is that kind of "Love thy neighbor" mentality that I hope continues. This situation has changed us, but I think in some ways for the better.

LET ME IN, LET ME IN, OR I WILL BLOW YOUR HOUSE DOWN

"Mami, next time let's build our playhouse out of bricks."

Youthful wisdom gained from the Three Little Pigs. My son is right. Hurricane Michael was the big, bad wolf trying to blow our house down—literally.

I sat our three sons in the tub of our downstairs bathroom. Then I heard my husband call from upstairs, asking for my help.

I handed my son a smoothie, his brother's bottle, and my cell phone and said, "You are in charge. Stay in here."

As I climbed the stairs, I found my husband bracing himself against the French doors that led out on to our balcony. He was using all of his weight to hold them shut, but they kept flying back open. I ran to hold the other door closed. It was a force like nothing I had ever felt before. My husband is a big man, and I had never seen anything physically move him like the wind did as it pushed against the doors.

LET ME IN, LET ME IN, OR I WILL BLOW YOUR HOUSE DOWN

We watched another door down the hall crumple like a piece of paper. We heard windows cracking. We were afraid that if we didn't hold these doors shut, the wind would rush in, lift the roof off, and destroy everything in it, including us.

We stayed there for about thirty minutes holding the doors. We shot each other desperate and defeated looks as I thought about our three children alone downstairs.

I wanted to go to them and make sure they were safe, but if I stopped holding the door, none of us would be safe.

After the worst of it had passed, I ran to the bathroom and found the boys crying. My sister was on the phone, singing to them to calm them down. They were terrified. We rode out the rest of the storm in the bathroom together. Our ears hurt from the changes in pressure. The walls shook and the doors jiggled. Thankfully, I gave our youngest a bottle, and he went to sleep.

When we finally emerged from the bathroom, there were waterfalls in our home. The upstairs was a mess.

We ran out of food and water after three days and so drove to Miami. We grew up in Miami and are used to hurricanes. This was unlike anything we had ever experienced.

We stayed with family and put the children in school to give them a sense of normalcy. The guidance counselors were amazing. They were very sensitive to the needs of our children, who were having a hard time sleeping and didn't want to be alone in the dark.

A little more than a month later, we left Miami and came back to Panama City. I wasn't sure it was the right thing to do. My children were adjusting well in Miami, and I didn't want to take that away from them, but I needed to help my husband manage the insurance claims and repairs on the house.

Once we got home, it was very clear that was the right decision. The children were so excited to see their friends and be back in their school.

Before bed one night, my son said, "Hurricane Michael needs to come back."

"Why?" I asked.

"He needs to apologize for all this mess."

We are helping our community clean up the mess and rebuild. It is important to us to be a part of that.

THE DIFFERENCE IS STARTLING

"Mom, you are driving right into the storm."

My son was half a world away but was tracking the hurricane as I drove home from a McDonald's Women Owners Network conference in Atlanta. I was hoping to make it home before the hurricane made landfall.

He was right. I pulled over in Eufaula and napped on the couch of a Hilton Garden Inn until a room was available.

I will never forget driving into Panama City the next day. It was a paralyzing feeling. The devastation was so complete that I missed turns that I had taken thousands of times. I got lost driving to my own home. I picked my way through downed power poles, transformers, trees, debris, and my neighbors' personal possessions.

That first night, we were totally shut off from the world. When you remove the light and sound of civilization, the difference is startling. I think many on the outside assumed no news was good news. That was a dangerous assumption. The sound of helicopters and sirens filled in the normal quiet spaces.

Our first objective was to account for our people and make sure they were safe. Social media was our lifeline for making those connections. Thankfully, everyone was safe, and we began doing what we could to get them back on their feet. A week after the storm, the McRig, the McDonald's semitruck version of a restaurant on wheels, was in the parking lot of the Panama City Mall giving out free and hot food to first responders and members of the community. A lot of people hadn't had a hot meal in days, and it gave people a chance to come together.

A hot meal is important, and so is a job and paycheck. Our son picked up ten thousand dollars in cash from friends in Tampa and drove it to Panama City so we could pay our folks in cash for the first four days they worked. All of the amazing people who came to work went home to their own personal destruction, loss, and damage.

I married into the McDonald's franchise business thirty-five years ago. My father-in-law opened up the first McDonald's in Bay County in 1962. This community is our home, and bringing our town back to life is our goal.

We lost half of our employees after the hurricane. People have hit the wall of tolerance. There is limited affordable housing. Transportation is a challenge. We have more business than we have people. It will take some time before our community is in a position to support the needs of the number of people required to do the work.

MEMOIRS OF MICHAEL: THE HURRICANE PROJECT

People ask if we are okay, and I honestly don't know. There is an uneasy and anxious ache inside. Sleep does not come easily. It's hard to turn your mind off from all this. My cure so far has been to work, be busy, restore our business, restore the lives of others, and restore our hometown. It is the only time I am not consumed with grief. We are humbled by the destruction and the aid we have received. What mattered so much a few months ago seems like foolishness today.

IT WAS THE LINEMEN

"We are bored! "I heard my two granddaughters call out as they sheltered in our small half bath.

"Just a little bit longer!"

My husband and son-in-law were holding the back doors shut while my daughter and I held the front door shut against nearly unstoppable wind.

My daughter and I took turns running around the house, grabbing buckets and bowls to catch the water, and using towels to sop up any that had already poured in. As the storm progressed, the chandelier in the foyer could double as a shower, as well as every light and air-conditioning vent.

After it passed, all of the neighbors in our cul-de-sac came out to inspect the damage. We already had a strong bond with our neighbors, but this brought us even closer.

One neighbor, who evacuated, had a freezer with an entire cow in it. They got word to us that we were welcome to eat it so it wouldn't go to waste. We dined well those first couple of nights.

We would cook dinner and eat together every night by lantern light after we had all put in a full day's work cleaning up the disaster Hurricane Michael had left behind.

I have sleep apnea and have to use a CPAP machine at night. Our wonderful neighbors, with a whole house generator, took in my family of six for six weeks. Their home was an oasis to us. To be able to work all day in the heat and humidity, and then walk into air-conditioning and a shower at night, is beyond words. We are forever humbled and grateful for their generosity.

I didn't cry over our destroyed home or the loss of our valuables. I didn't shed a tear over the family vacation to Colorado we couldn't go on or the cancelled cruise.

It was the linemen, the truck after truck after truck filled with linemen from all over the country pouring into our weary and ravaged community to give us power, that brought tears to my eyes.

They missed birthdays, anniversaries, and holidays so I could flip a switch and have a little bit of normal restored. They

initially estimated it would take up to three months to get power. We had power in nine days. It was amazing.

We have two trailers in our driveway now, one for my husband and me, and one for my daughter and her family. The contractors are estimating that our house could take up to a year to repair.

NO DAMSELS IN DISTRESS HERE

My daughter was worried, and she asked me to evacuate with her. I told her the nursing license I carry means that I have a responsibility to stay and take care of my patients.

After I finished my shift that day, I came home to pack my overnight bag. My husband said, "If you are staying, I am staying too."

We sent our daughter to New Orleans to be with her brothers and our extended family. I packed my bag and drove to Community Health and Rehab to spend the night. I figured I would be home the next afternoon.

I set up my air mattresses in the lobby and watched the news coverage with the other nurses and staff who were spending the night. No one got any real sleep. Everyone was awake and working by 4:00 a.m. My husband arrived shortly before the winds started to pick up to ride out the storm with me.

There were 115 patients in the facility. Most were mature adults who were receiving long-term care or rehab after a surgery or illness.

We knew we needed to stay ahead of the game. We started preparing lunch early to ensure everyone was fed before the storm hit. We pulled patients into the hallway and away from windows, as a precaution.

Then I heard it. It sounded like someone shuffling a deck of cards. It was the shingles flying off the roof. Then the water started pouring in. The winds intensified, and the boarding on the windows blew off. The exterior doors blew open, and debris started flying into the building.

Every free hand grabbed a wheelchair or a bed and started moving patients to the opposite wing of the building. It was a massive train of people dodging debris. We got to the end of the hall, and the ceiling fell in. The train of people turned around and started moving in the other direction to find a safe place to ride out the storm.

Then another door blew open. More debris flew in. Anything hanging on the walls was ripped down by the wind.

Every room had water pouring in except the therapy room. We brought everyone into that room and continued to provide care. A stressful situation can cause blood pressure to rise and can cause someone to have a heart attack. We needed to prevent that from happening.

From the therapy room, we had a clear view of everything that was going on. All of the remaining windows blew in. Glass and rain covered everything.

Miraculously, during all of this, I had cell reception. My director asked that I call 911. It wasn't to ask for help but to tell them we were here. The situation had deteriorated, and we didn't think we were going to make it.

I called the operator and told them how many people were in the facility and where they could find us after the storm passed.

Another nurse was sharing her Sharpie so people could write their information on their arms to help the first responders identify their bodies. She handed it to me, but I couldn't do it. It was an act of defeat. I wasn't ready to give up.

I was able to get a call through to my son in New Orleans. He was able to tell me that we were in the outer eye wall. The eye would not pass over us, so we wouldn't get a break. We still had an hour to go.

My husband and two other men were trying to hold shut the fire doors. The wind would easily push them open and slam the doors shut again. I was afraid someone was going to get hurt, but they kept holding them as best they could.

The winds shifted, and the rest of the windows blew in. Through the phone, my three children could hear the chaos. They knew it was bad. I told them I didn't know what was going to happen. I didn't think this building was going to hold. It was an emotionally detached conversation. It had to be, or I would have broken down. I didn't have time for that.

We felt the winds die down a bit. I got back on the phone with my son and asked if it was over. It felt like it was. It was gut-wrenching to hear him say another big band was coming any second now.

About fifteen minutes, later the worst was over. Reality set in. We were stuck. We had no place to take the patients, and help wasn't coming any time soon. Nearly everything and everybody was wet. Somehow the linen closet stayed mostly dry. We got patients changed into dry clothes and put dry sheets on the beds.

Once the winds died down completely, I walked outside. There was a train on the tracks knocked over on its side. Power lines and trees covered the roads. It was silent and eerie.

Over the next forty-eight hours, the staff took turns caring for patients and taking naps in our cars in the parking lot.

Eventually buses arrived to take the patients to new facilities out of town. It was hard. These were my patients, and I would never know whether they were going to be okay. It was like sending a family member away. The last bus drove away at midnight two days after the storm hit.

They were leaving on a bus and not in an ambulance. No one got hurt or sick—or died. That is a testament to how hard the staff worked.

I drove home the next morning dodging trees and power lines. I had to drive only three miles, but I wasn't sure where I was going. None of the landmarks were there.

When I pulled into the driveway, my son's friend was there, asking if my son was home and if he needed a job. There was a roofing company that was hiring.

I told him, "I need a job. Do you think they would hire a nurse?"

In addition to losing my job, we lost the income from two rental homes. We have one kid in college and another going next year. Not having a job wasn't an option. I cleaned up and went to their recently established mobile office on Twenty-third Street to apply.

They gave me a job doing project management and sales. It's been a learning curve. I had to get smart on the laws and codes and the product line, but I am figuring it out. You do what you have to do to make life work.

NEXT STOP, DISNEY WORLD

I had my triceratops stuffed animal and my blanket with me. I tried to take a nap, but my sister kept waking me up. It is hard to sleep on the bathroom floor while a hurricane is outside. My mom and dad let us watch at first. The trees fell, and then the gazebo. After that, they made us go into the bathroom.

We could hear the swirling sounds. Then water started pouring in from the vents. After it was over, my dad got us out of the bathroom. He put my sister on his shoulders, my mom held my hand, and we went outside.

We saw that there was water in the road. It was as high as the tire on the car that was parked in the road. Trees and street lights were down.

The next day, we explored all the trees and limbs that were down. We would jump from tree to tree and pretend like we were monkeys. We made a game out of everything that Hurricane Michael left behind. There were some leftover bricks, and we built an animal town. We had an animal hotel, and an animal church. We even had an animal jail.

My pop-pop had to cut up the trees we were playing on, without us knowing. We cried. He said he would take us to Disney World and get us an Avatar toy there. We can't wait to go!

CONFEDERATE COMPASSION

Chris

"Any chance I could hire you to board up my windows?" I asked my neighbor, who was boarding up his house. I am a lawyer. That isn't one of my skill sets.

I had spent the day before the hurricane filling forty sandbags. We thought the storm surge was going to be our biggest problem. It wasn't until I saw my neighbor's preparation that I might need to consider the damage the wind could cause.

My wife and I were playing UNO with my seventy-five-year-old mother and our seven-year-old daughter when the power went out. Once the winds

picked up, we moved into the master bedroom closet. Three adults, two dogs, and one child. It was close quarters.

To pass the time, we turned on some music and belted "Bohemian Rhapsody" at the top of our lungs. Then we could start to feel the pressure change. I stood by the bedroom door and watched our entire home get destroyed.

One upstairs window blew out, and it was like a vacuum that sucked the rest of the house with it. Then the eye passed over, and everything got incredibly quiet.

Michele

My wife took my face in her hands and said, "When you go out there, I need you to remember these are just material things. You wanted to remodel anyway. We will be okay."

When I walked out and saw the destruction, I almost lost it. Tears filled my eyes. We didn't have much time to wander around. It was lunchtime, and I needed to hurry to the kitchen to make peanut butter and jelly sandwiches. My hands were shaking so bad I could hardly make them.

I found my daughter's walkie-talkie radio and scrolled through the channels until we heard a man's voice. He gave his street address. He was one house away. We looked out across the street and could see our neighbor talking into his radio.

"Are you all okay?" he asked.

We told him we were. This was the first time we had ever spoken to our neighbor.

The Confederate flag he flew outside his home every day led us to believe that we wouldn't see eye to eye on a lot of issues. We waved to him one last time before we headed back into our closet for the back half of the storm.

CONFEDERATE COMPASSION

Chris

My mother spent the better part of the storm praying in Spanish. Hurricane Maria devastated her home in Puerto Rico in 2017. Now she was watching Hurricane Michael do the same to her home in Panama City.

After the storm had passed and it was safe to leave the closet, I knew we had to prepare our daughter for what she was about to see.

I said, "Remember the movie *Sing*? When the theater crashed down and the Koala was sad and depressed?"

It clicked with her. You could see it on her seven-year-old face. She walked out and said, "Yup, this is just like *Sing*."

It helped that her room, the garage, and our room were intact. The other side of the house was destroyed but could be replaced.

That night, my wife cooked a hot meal using tea lights and a grill screen. The canned spaghetti was the best meal I have ever had.

We slept that night in the two bedrooms that were not destroyed. The silence was deafening. The silence and all the beeping fire alarms.

Michele

The next morning, we sat outside and ate cereal in the back of our SUV so that we could listen to the radio. A Discovery Channel television crew came walking through our neighborhood. One man, from the Cajun Navy, had a cell phone that worked. We called everyone we could think of, but no one was answering the phone. We finally got hold of a friend who was able to let everyone else know we were safe.

With a seven-year-old and a seventy-five-year-old, we knew we couldn't stay. We decided to go to Tallahassee. Our Confederate flag neighbors across the street helped us pull off the garage door that had blown in so we could get our second car out of the garage.

We offered them all the food that was in our home. After we left, they kept watch over our house. They even pulled a gun on a would-be looter. It was reassuring to know our possessions were being looked after.

Despite our differences, we are taking care of each other. I wish it didn't take a hurricane to stop us in our tracks and redefine what is important in life.

MY HURRICANE BFF

We evacuated to Birmingham, Alabama. The hotel room was really small. My dog peed on the carpet. She snuck into the bag of sugar cookies and ate them. Then she got sick. We were all getting on each other's nerves.

My parents wouldn't let me go back into Panama City with them after the hurricane. They said it was too dangerous. We simply wanted to see our house and find out whether our play house and trampoline were okay. They said no.

We had to go to a new school. I overheard my new teacher saying that I wear the same outfit every day. We didn't pack a lot of my clothes when we evacuated from Panama City. I asked my mom to buy me some new clothes. She did.

A friend from my old school got to be in my class at my new school. We did everything together. Ate lunch together. Played Frisbee at recess together. One time, I threw the Frisbee over the fence, and the teachers never found out. We were friends before, but now we are best friends.

My parents told me we get to move home. I am happy and I am sad. I missed the Thanksgiving performance at my old school, and now I am going to miss the spring musical performance at my new school. I sobbed the night we left. I hated leaving my friend at that school all by herself. She needs me. I am the only one there who knows what it is like to be in a hurricane.

HURRICANE CLOSET

We had the wine ready.

My sister and her family lived in Panama City Beach and came to ride out the storm with us at our house in Panama City. We figured we would lose power, but that would be the worst of it.

The night before the storm, we rode around town to see if everyone had evacuated. They hadn't. Everyone was still at home. My husband told me I was being nervous for no reason.

The day of the hurricane, we slept until 9:00 a.m. The lights began to flicker at 11:30. Then the windows started shaking. We were scared, but I didn't want the kids to see how scared we were. We heard a sound like a faucet running. It was water pouring into the kitchen.

We all crammed into a small closet. There were seven people and two dogs in that tiny closet. The normally active dogs were completely still. I prayed and asked God to save us. I told him that I would be a better person.

HURRICANE CLOSET

My brother-in-law had cell phone reception, and his friend was sending weather updates. We still had a long time to go until the storm passed.

My husband grabbed a twin mattress and placed it in front of the closet doors to protect us. The water was rising around us. We were cold, wet, and scared. Then part of the roof came off. We told the kids not to look up. We covered their heads in case something fell on us.

After it was over, we all went out and got into my husband's truck. From that vantage point, we could see the utter destruction. Our entire roof had come off except the roof over the tiny closet in which we were hiding. Incredible, right? God answered our prayers that day.

We sat in the truck and cried. All of us.

More of our neighbors came outside. We began going door to door and checking on people. We stayed the first night with a neighbor. Their house was almost untouched. It is hard to understand why some had total devastation and others didn't.

My sister's house in Panama City Beach was fine, so we stayed with her.

We needed to uphold the promise we'd made to God that day. My husband and I began volunteering at our church, St. Dominic's. They are the only Catholic church in Panama City that offers a Spanish mass. This storm was especially hard for the Spanish-speaking community. The Catholic Church and Catholic charities made sure everyone received help no matter what.

We spent every day after the storm volunteering. On Sundays we partnered with the Spanish community and donated all the hot meals to Hurricane Michael victims. Parishioners and nonparishioners. Anyone who showed up who needed a warm meal. It was a beautiful thing to be there, helping others.

I believe it was because of our commitment to helping others and our faith in God that we were able to settle with FEMA pretty early on.

We needed a place to stay because my husband and I both had to go back to work. There was an advertisement on Facebook for a town home. It was too good to be true. It had to be a scam.

We showed up thirty minutes before the open house was scheduled to begin. There were ten other families there waiting to be interviewed as well. The owner was a single mom who was in the military and was being reassigned. She interviewed us and decided we could rent her home. I couldn't believe. She is a blessing to us.

Now we are focused on helping others as much as we can. We all want to get back to normal.

RANGER RICK AND THE RED RIDER WAGON

After the gazebo fell, it got real. The front door was bouncing off the hinges. The chimney came off and landed by the back door.

This was my husband's first hurricane, and it was proving to be very eventful.

I have lived in Panama City since I was in the first grade. After having kids, we moved back so we could be closer to family. We had spent the long weekend in Panama City Beach with my husband's family. We weren't worried at all. It was only going to be a category one or two. We would be fine.

We had some friends who had to evacuate at the last minute, so the morning before the storm, I drove over to pick up their dog. Now we had six people and five dogs in the house. We set up chairs and watched the Hurricane Michael show—until the water started pouring in. Then we were running around the house and trying to catch water with pots, pans, buckets, and trash cans. We are still trying to figure out who grabbed the spaghetti strainer to catch the water.

We were sopping wet and didn't have time to be scared.

It's amazing how much strength you have when you know the only thing that's stopping a door from being blown in is you.

After it was over, we wanted to check on a friend's house nearby. We waded down the middle of the road, dodging debris in hip-high water. We got to their house, picked up their cat, and grabbed some important documents that they didn't take. They assumed they would be gone for a few days, not weeks. Their daughter had a Red Rider wagon, and we filled it to the top with their belongings. The wagon floated behind us as we made the journey back home. In case you were counting, at this point we were up to six people, five dogs, and a cat.

In the days after the storm, it was nice not having cell phone service or connectivity. We weren't worried about the outside world. We were focused on taking care of our neighbors and each other. The neighbors starting calling my husband Ranger Rick. He had two guns on his hips to deter looters. It worked.

This experience revealed everyone's true character. You can't be fake when you don't have power or water and are blind with exhaustion from working all day.

One of our grumpy neighbors was mowing his lawn the next day. We couldn't believe it. Gas was a precious commodity, and we felt like he was wasting it.

For now, we are in a camper in my parents' driveway. We are looking to buy a house, but it's challenging. Some houses need to be repaired, but most construction loans require the work to be completed in six months. No contractors can guarantee that at this point.

I am thankful my family is safe. I am thankful we were here to help my parents catch water, rip up carpet, and prevent the damage from being worse than it was. One of the most humbling feelings has been longtime friends reaching out to ask if we are okay. It makes you stop and realize that people really do care.

GOD'S LESSON: HUMILITY AND PRIDE

My dad has always been a talker and storyteller. He has a knack for embellishing the way any fisherman does. After a fishing trip, we would always ask ourselves whether the fish that got away was really as big as he said it was.

"Your back porch just ripped off," he said mid-hurricane in the few sporadic calls we got from him during the storm. We weren't entirely sure whether we could believe him.

He had come over to our house the night before the storm. My parents' house was in a flood zone, and my mom was out of town.

The later in the evening it got, the more nervous I became. The weatherman on television was crying. We had a friend in the emergency operations center, and his voice changed. He wasn't calm anymore.

I couldn't shake this anxious feeling in my gut, and we made the decision. We were leaving. I packed for six people in five minutes.

We woke up our children and piled them into the van. My dad said he was staying.

We drove away from the house but turned around, went back, and asked him one last time to leave with us. Nope. He was staying.

We drove to my brother's house in Pensacola. He doesn't usually answer his phone late at night, but that night he did.

After the hurricane, my dad said, "Your house is in pretty bad shape."

When we were finally able to get back in, "bad shape" was an understatement. We had over fifty trees down. My husband's truck had a tree on it. A third of our roof and trusses had come off, and there was water everywhere in the house. The entire front door insert was lying down on the front porch. The back door had blown in, and the hurricane had blown right through the middle of our house.

Later, we would learn my husband's office was destroyed, and my parents' home would also have to be torn down.

One of the last memories I had was

a baby doll in my daughter's crib. It was now covered in insulation. The lawn looked like yellow snow because the insulation was everywhere.

When our neighbors saw my dad emerge from the house, they were shocked to find out that someone was inside. They offered for him to stay with them, but he refused. I think he felt the need to protect his little girl's home. He hooked his CPAP machine up to a boat battery and slept soaking wet downstairs.

Most of our belongings in our house were destroyed. Toys, clothes, and books—all gone. My sister-in-law had written little notes in the books she had given my children as gifts. She died suddenly last summer. Losing these irreplaceable things are the hardest.

My daughter asked why we didn't save more of her things. My son told me one night after I tucked him in that he was homesick and wanted to be back in his room.

As a mother, those questions break your heart.

At the end of the day, it is just stuff. It was simply shocking to lose it in that manner.

The first insurance adjuster didn't even walk into our house. He stood outside and said it was a total loss. Another adjuster said that it could be salvaged. The next adjuster came with a structural engineer and agreed with the first: there was nothing left to save, and they would have to wipe it off the foundation. Financially, we are not going to come out on top after all this. It will cost us twice the amount to rebuild our house to what it was before. The cost of supplies and labor has increased drastically, and the time lines are months longer.

My husband and I were born and raised in Panama City, and we won't leave. Too much of our life is here. This has always been the kind of town that takes care of people, or maybe it is just the people with whom I surround myself. Our family and friends (both here and out of town) were amazing. They helped us box up what we could salvage, cut trees in our yard, and find a rental house. They arranged for our kids to have new mattresses, and their kids shared their own toys and clothes. They brought us sheets, towels, and meals, and they kept our kids when we needed to work at the house or meet insurance adjusters.

A friend helped me dig through knee-deep insulation just to find a painting of our house my son had done in kindergarten. It has an even deeper meaning to me now.

We wouldn't have been able to make it through all this without them and our faith in God. I would much prefer to be on the giving end of generosity instead of the receiving end, but sometimes God wants to teach you about humility, pride, and accepting help. It has been a difficult time, but we know that God is faithful and has already provided for us so much.

THE HURRICANE IS COMING, RIGHT MEOW

When it became a category four, we had no choice. We had to stay. We wouldn't have left the cats though. We take in rescued cats, and there are too many to pile into a car.

We stayed for Opal. We didn't think this would be much different. We bought supplies and waited for the storm.

Once the winds start rattling the house, we propped a mattress up against the windows and pushed a dresser up against it to hold it in place.

We watched television with our granddaughter until the power went out. Luckily, my daughter had charged her iPad, and she was able to play games on that.

My husband, my daughter, and I watched the trees on our property line bend, sway, and eventually snap. Water starting pouring in from every light fixture. The ceiling in our bedroom fell in.

The wind died down, and the eye passed over us. It was eerie and quiet. The cats did okay, hiding and huddling together.

A lot of our cats have health issues—feline AIDS, leukemia. There is an apartment complex behind our house, and most of cats are abandoned after people move away. We take them in. One cat, Bashful, has a heart condition. We were afraid the stress from the hurricane would kill him. We made sure he had his medication, and he did fine.

The damage after the storm was surreal. We relied on our neighbors to get through those tough days after the storm. We shared food and water. We couldn't have made it without them.

My granddaughter did well during the hurricane but is now bothered by sound of strong winds, especially at night.

I feel like the rest of the country has forgotten about us. Once they heard that Panama City Beach, the spring break capital of the world, was up and running, they moved on. The east side of Bay County is still in shambles.

As for us, we will rebuild. We will make the improvements on the house so we can get back to normal. I would love to have a room on the back of the house for the cats, where they can see outside without having to be outside. We want to do more for them and show them that people care.

BE A BLESSING

"Our friend fired you."

The four words were like little razor blades slicing my skin in the most sensitive areas. The corner of my eyes. Between each of my fingers.

It is a small town, and I knew that anything I said would be repeated, exaggerated, and then repeated again. Even my facial expressions would be put under cross-examination. I simply smiled and stood there until I was able to find a break in the conversation and walk away.

The truth hurts. But I am not sure I was fired. They clearly didn't want me, but was I fired? I was offered a job before the hurricane. Every day after the storm, I waited to hear when they wanted me to start. They eventually called, but it didn't go as I expected. The job was no longer available. I lost my home, my car, and now my job. I was hurt and mad. Mad at first, and then later hurt. I drank too much. I made a lot of snide comments. Then I made a lot of self-deprecating comments. My pride was wounded. Sometimes it takes a painful experience to make us change our ways. I began to take stock of my flaws. Outspoken, but hard working. Arrogant, but organized. Unforgiving.

Clearly, I wasn't perfect, and I needed to change.

My pastor talked about holding stones. We can throw them at people, or we can use them to build an altar to pray.

I couldn't let this disappointment rot my insides and cause poison to fall from my tongue. I prayed a lot for forgiveness, guidance, wisdom, and patience.

I got back out there. I did what I know how to do. And it worked. I am back on feet and have landed in a great place.

Hurricane Michael destroyed a lot of things in my life, but it made way for new things. A better version of my life.

I didn't get to this place on my own. My family and my faith got me here. Instead of being the best, now I hope to be a blessing.

BE A BLESSING

HIS GRACE

As I scroll through the pictures now, the ones my son took while we huddled under a conference room table at the Lynn Haven police station, I am in awe.

This is the hurricane through his eyes. It will one day be a part of his testimony. Pictures of people praying. Strangers at the time, but now family. He was so brave.

My son insisted on wearing his SWAT gear police costume. My husband is a Lynn Haven police officer, and my son wants to be just like him. My husband was on mandatory duty during the hurricane, and we decided to ride out the storm with him at the police department.

The night before the storm, we slept on the floor in his office, or tried to, while my husband and his fellow officers did everything they could to prepare for the storm. We have three children, ages five, two, and seven months. The next morning, we stood in the commission hall with the other families that had come to ride out the storm. It was an old church steeple attached to the building with large windows and glass doors. We looked outside and saw the rain pouring down sideways and trees bending and snapping in half.

The lights would flicker on and off. The glass windows began to rattle and shake. We retreated into the training room of the police department. We were sitting up against a wall and we heard loud booms and things hitting the building. It was the windows of the steeple on the other side of the wall being sucked out.

A girl we had just met was holding my seven-month-old daughter while I tried to entertain our five-year-old and two-year-old so they wouldn't be frightened. I remember looking over and watching her cover my daughter's head as the sound rang through our ears. Her reflexes were so parental and protective.

The glass shattered, and the large air-conditioning vents ripped off of the roof.

The wind ripped through the building. The air was thick and we could smell diesel fuel. Our ears were popping because of the continuous pressure changes. The wall started to crumble. We shuffled down the hallway to my husband's office. I and our three children got under his desk. Then the roof ripped off, and water started pouring in. His computer was still plugged in, and all I could think of was that we were going to be electrocuted. My husband ran in the room and ripped the cords out of the wall.

We moved again to a new conference room and crammed ourselves under the large table. There were ten people sitting shoulder to shoulder, some panicking and crying hysterically. During this truly traumatic event, my five-year-old son seemed to be somewhat calm. He took pictures and played songs from his vacation Bible school that I had saved on my phone.

He would show videos to everyone. I think it took our minds off what was going on outside, and it helped everyone in the room. He was so brave.

It seemed as if the hurricane would never let up. We were in the outer wall of the hurricane for almost four hours and never received relief from the eye. It became more and more intense, and the roof was lifting up and down. I began to think that we might not make it out of here.

Finally, around 4:00 p.m., the winds let down. It was over, and we were able open the doors to the outside. It was such a relief.

I have never seen my husband on the job before. Once it was safe, I watched all of the police officers jump into action. One couldn't help but be caught up in their energy to go out and help. They put on raincoats and jumped on four-wheelers and side-by-sides. Others were on foot to canvas the town, check on the damage, and search for people.

The officers did everything they could do to clear a path to get in and out of the immediate area. None of the officers' radios worked, and nobody's phones worked. My husband and I had cell phones with AT&T service, which we gave up to all of the city officials to use to get in touch with the emergency operations center.

My husband came back to the police station around 7:30 p.m. and told me we were moving to the Southerland Event Center. The city commissioner and his family helped me load up the kids and our personal items into my truck. My husband, driving a side-by-side, escorted us to the Southerland Event Center for shelter. I couldn't believe what I saw during that short drive. Trees, debris, power poles, and water—it looked like a war zone. Our town was destroyed.

We set up cots when we arrived, but no one could really sleep.

The Saturday after the storm, we needed to find somewhere else to go. The Southerland Event Center was needed for other purposes. As we drove through the city of Lynn Haven and Panama City, all one could see was destruction. It was about 6:00 p.m. when we approached the Hathaway Bridge. In front of me, I could start to see street lights and businesses illuminating the drive, but when I looked in my rearview mirror, it was pitch-black.

We finally made it to one of the only hotels open in the area. My husband made sure his guys were checked in and then unloaded our belongings only to find out this place was not livable and was crawling with roaches. This is the moment that I broke down. All of it hit me at once, and I could not help but cry.

I called my grandmother and cried. So many relatives poured love into my family after the storm. They combined their resources and rented a clean place for us to stay in Destin. My husband was making the four-hour round-trip drive between Destin and Panama City six days a week. He said it was worth it to keep our babies in suitable living conditions.

On my husband's first day off since the storm, he said we needed a touch of normalcy, and he was craving a steak.

We sat at our table at Longhorn Steakhouse discussing our post-hurricane plans and the conversations we'd had with our insurance company. When we were finished, we asked for our bill, and our waiter told us a woman, who had overheard us talking, had paid our bill. My husband was overwhelmed with gratitude, and he cried right there in the steakhouse. I have never really seen him cry before, except maybe during the birth of our children. It was a simple act of kindness, but it was a vibrant reminder of God showing us his grace—the grace that we had experienced many times over the last few days.

We had made it out alive. His grace.

The kids were okay. His grace.

We had a place to live. His grace.

Now, a free steak dinner. Definitely His grace.

We have had three adjusters and two inspectors at our house. The progress is slow. It is humbling to realize how little you can actually live with. We don't actually need all of the things we accumulate. This situation has definitely tested us, but there is so much positive that has and will continue to come from it.

CAN I BORROW YOUR BIKE?

I decided to turn off the TV because the weather channel wasn't doing me any good. I had made the decision to stay, and there wasn't any changing that.

The hour before the storm made landfall was exceptionally uneventful. There were no more preparations to make, just unsettled waiting.

While looking south over the water on St. Andrew's Bay, I could see the storm approaching. Even though the storm was still miles away, the most disturbing part at that point was the roar of the wind. It was like a fleet of helicopters barreling toward our town, and there was no possible change of course.

My wife had taken the kids to Tuscaloosa. We joked before the storm that it would be just bad enough to knock out power to give her an extra day off and a good excuse to go to the Alabama football game that Saturday.

The three of them were safe and away from the storm. I needed to stay to make sure that if something happened to our house or my wife's business, I could remedy it immediately to further reduce any damages. My wife is an owner of a business, and we were in the process of buying a new building. We had three buildings in Hurricane Michael's path. My goal was to get everything back to normal before my family made it back to town.

I anxiously watched as the rain bands began to hit the windows. When the first trees started to fall in the yard, my cell phone still had service. Even though I was in contact with my family, I chose not to let them know trees were starting to fall.

Trees falling meant things were getting bad. I didn't want them to know things were getting bad. I knew it was time to hunker down when debris started to fly horizontally across the yard. Our two dogs and I nestled into our area of safety in the laundry room. As the storm raged, I could feel the house shaking, and the sound of a freight train filled the air. Before cell service went out, my wife sent me a chart that showed the expected timeline of the storm. When I felt the storm intensifying, I looked at the chart. Two more hours to go.

I closed my eyes and imagined I was on a turbulent airplane that would soon land. That all changed when the smoke alarms activated. My first thought was, *Oh, my gosh, my house is burning down in the middle of a hurricane.*

In fact, the alarms were sounding because a cascade of water was pouring into the house and right through what seemed like every vent and light socket. I spent the last two hours of the storm using every trash can, storage bin, ice cooler, pot, and pan to catch as much water as I could. It felt like a futile exercise because every time I dumped one bucket out, another was already overflowing. I couldn't just sit idle—I had to do something to try to save our home.

The storm passed, and I went outside for the first time. It felt ironic that the weather turned into a beautiful day. The front yard had at least twenty trees down, but luckily none had hit the house. As the sun was starting to set, I made my preparations for the night to come with no power.

I made dinner with some food we had left in the fridge. I mopped up the floors and hung wet towels out to dry. Little did I know that in a week, the floors and walls that I worked hard to keep dry would be taken down to the subfloor and the studs.

Back in Tuscaloosa, my wife was watching the news coverage. She saw the flattened buildings on Twenty-third Street, very close to her office. She had it worse than I did. I knew that I was fine, but she didn't. Everything she was seeing made her doubt my well-being.

I heard someone beating on my front door. I knew looting would be a concern. The front door was jammed shut from the storm and didn't open anymore, so I went to the side door. I opened it to find our friend who lived a over a mile away. My wife had gotten in touch with him, and he had hiked for hours to get to my house to check on me. I have so much appreciation that he would come that far for me.

His phone had reception, but the battery died before he got to my house. I supplied him with a flashlight, and he began the trek back to his house. It took him several hours to get back in the dark but when he did, he was able to charge his phone and get a message back to my wife that I was safe. She said those were the worst twelve hours of her life.

The next morning, I needed to get out of the neighborhood to check on our office buildings. I had taken a survival course the year before, so the next morning I packed a bag that would have made the survival instructors proud.

I put on my running shoes and started the five-mile trek across town to Twenty-third Street. I passed a neighbor who said, "Where are you running to?"

My reply was simple: "I have places I need to get to."

I stopped at a friend's house. No one was home, so I tossed a note inside the house through a broken window to let them know I was fine.

I ran past McKenzie Park and saw an American flag, torn and battered, lying on the ground. I folded it up and put it in my backpack. The flag deserved to be preserved after what we all had been through. I kept running. I passed a group of people on bikes. I offered them one hundred dollars to buy a bike. They said no.

I asked a guy in a pickup truck for a lift. He dropped me off a mile shy of my destination. He also had a bike in the bed of his truck. I offered to buy his bike for one hundred dollars. He said no.

I ran the rest of the way to the building we were in the process of buying. It did well. We were lucky. I still needed a way to get around town. I stopped at an apartment complex to find a group of residents standing outside. I asked again if I could buy a bike.

As I expected, one resident said I couldn't buy their bike but then surprised me by saying I could borrow it for as long as I needed, free of charge.

The bike had character. Instead of brakes, I had to drag my feet on the ground to come to a stop. It wouldn't have won any races, but it got me around town for the next several days.

I made it to my wife's current office. Total destruction. The roof was gone, and every room had a collapsed ceiling. There wasn't anything I could do to mitigate the damage, so I secured what I could, put the backup hard drives in my backpack, and moved on.

I stopped at the hospital and convinced the security guards to let me make a phone call. It was a short call to my wife to let her know I was okay, the house had water in it, the old office was gone, but the new office was fine. Her response was simple. "Okay,

I'm coming to help." She coordinated for our children to stay with their grandmother and made the drive into Panama City.

Over the next several days, my wife and I would work from sun up to sun down to clean up what we could.

We heard that the Toyota dealership was giving out hot food. As we were waiting in line, my wife looked at me and said, "We should be the ones helping."

In most situations, we are fortunate enough to be able to help and give to others. Right now, we didn't have any food to eat ourselves. It was a humbling moment. Everyone had been set back to the same point.

Six days after the storm, we drove to Walton County to celebrate my wife's birthday. We all needed a break from our new reality, and this offered us a few hours of normalcy.

Grandma drove the kids down from North Carolina. It was the first time I had seen our two children since before the storm. Our embrace seemed to last for an eternity. No one wanted to let go. My wife snapped a picture. To most people, it would look like any other family photo, but it wasn't just a normal photo. It was something more.

Our children have been relentlessly resilient through it all. As we drive through town and pass the destruction, they have turned into mini property appraisers. "Damaged. Severely damaged. Oh, that one is a total loss."

We are slowly getting our lives back together. There are good days and bad days, but progress is being made.

The company I work for was flexible with my schedule those first few weeks after the storm.

Three months after the storm, I returned the borrowed bike to the rightful owner. I was grateful for that generosity.

After four months of construction, my wife's office opened to rave reviews in her new location. Now we are focused on home repairs.

The storm seemed to take away so much, and getting back to our daily routine is an important aspect of pursuing my new goals. Normalcy and happiness. These goals seem simple, but nowadays most people in our area can likely appreciate that they are hard to obtain.

HOLD YOUR HORSES

I was too worried about my horses to say much to my sister, who was crammed into a small closet with me during the hurricane. I had thirty-six horses on the property, and seven of them were pregnant. We breed and train national championship Arabian horses.

There are many expert opinions on what to do with horses during a hurricane. Some say to keep them in the barn. There is the risk that if the barn is destroyed, it could injure or kill them. Other people suggest keeping them all outside, but once your fences are down, they could wander into a nearby road and be hit by a car.

I moved thirty of the horses into the barn while the other six, who are used to being outside, stayed in the pasture. They had spent the last eighteen years in the pasture, and they would be better there than forced into barn stalls.

Before the hurricane hit, I filled up their stalls with food and water and tagged each horse with my contact information in case they wandered off.

My sister had evacuated from her home in Lynn Haven to my parents' farm in Southport. They have a brick house on thirty acres. We thought we would be safer the farther away we were from the water.

We stocked up on food and water, and I ensured we had two weeks of food for the horses at the farm and another two months' worth of food at a warehouse in Panama City.

Our house is two hundred feet from the barn, but during the hurricane, the wind obstructed the view. When we watched the chimney land in the pool, we knew it was time to take shelter.

MEMOIRS OF MICHAEL: THE HURRICANE PROJECT

Shingles ripped off the roof, and water poured in through the nineteen-foot ceilings as my parents sat in the downstairs bathroom. My sister, three poodles, and I were in a closet across the hallway from them.

I was surrounded by my show clothes, the beautiful tailored coats and shirts that I would wear when I would show my horse in competition. The National Championship was in a week. Would I be able to show my horse?

Water started pouring into the closet. The clothes were destroyed. We have one poodle that we call queen of the farm, and she didn't want to get her feet wet, so she sat on my shoulders.

It was hot in the closet, especially with a dog on my shoulders. Miraculously, we had cell service and were able to get storm updates from our sister in Washington State and a friend in Colorado.

When the winds died down, I went outside to check on the horses. They were all safe. Not a scratch on any of them. The horse barns survived, but my work barn and the hay barns were destroyed.

The work barn fell on our backhoe, and the work horse tractor was covered in metal roofing and debris. A neighbor came over and cut fourteen trees off the driveway so we could get a car out.

I went to the barn for the first time after the storm. There were eight trees down in between the house and the barn. I had to climb over and under trees just to get there. The front doors of one barn were ripped off and on the ground. The doors of the other barn were damaged so badly by the force of the wind that they were almost impossible to open.

My sister left to check on my parents' business and her house in Panama City, and I began to feed and water the horses.

Horses drink five to ten gallons of water a day on average. Our whole house generator was destroyed, and we were without power and water. I moved about 360 gallons of water from the pond to the barn with one small wheelbarrow.

Dr. Bess Darrow, a veterinarian and equine dentist from Ocala, brought us medications for the horses and arranged for someone else to foster my horses while we cleaned up the farm. I have never met the people who cared for my horses for four months after the hurricane.

I wasn't able to compete in the competition after the storm. My trainer showed my horse for me, and he won a Reserve National Championship.

We are still in recovery mode.

Nothing in our home was salvageable. We have had four insurance adjustors come out, but we haven't heard from any of them since November. The mitigator billed the insurance company directly, but they haven't been paid them. They may put a lien on the property.

This hurricane has been a big hit. The horse-breeding business is a large financial investment, and none of it is covered by insurance. We are trying to figure out where the money will come from.

Not having the arenas to train the horses means we have to pay to send them off to be trained. This is five times more expensive than if I did it myself.

We have eight babies due anytime now. We need to breed at least four more mares this year so we have something to sell four years from now. We can't afford to miss a year.

There will be lots of changes as we figure out what we really need to operate. It won't look exactly like it did before, but we are working hard to put life back together.

TREE HOUSE

"Why don't they take the tree off their house?"

An innocent question that will reveal all of the ugliness of the adult world.

I want to say, "Life isn't fair. Even if you are a good person and you work hard, a hurricane can come through and wipe out everything you have."

I want to say, "Social inequality is prevalent, and we need to do what we can to help each other."

I want to say, "Use your talents for good and make a difference. Whatever they are, find a way to make a positive impact in the world."

I want to say all those things, but I don't. It is a weighty topic for a seven-year-old on a Monday morning.

This event will be a defining moment of her childhood. As an adult, she will look back with utter disgust that it took our government over two hundred days to provide a disaster relief bill. She will recall the countless volunteers that provided backpacks to her school and helped tarp roofs. Any spots in her memory or questions she has, I will be able to fill in. Today, I want to keep her innocent for just a little bit longer.

"That is a great question, sweetie. Let's say a prayer that they get the help they need to fix their house."

LOVE

I am learning to love things that aren't new and beautiful.

    That is what the hurricane taught me.

    The battered and weary among us have endured more after this storm than some will endure in a lifetime.

    We need a little extra love.

www.ingramcontent.com/pod-product-compliance
Lightning Source LLC
Chambersburg PA
CBHW041123300426
44113CB00002B/39